CHILDREN'S STORYTELLERS

Charles Schulz

by Kari Schuetz

BELLWETHER MEDIA · MINNEAPOLIS, MN

Note to Librarians, Teachers, and Parents:

Blastoff! Readers are carefully developed by literacy experts and combine standards-based content with developmentally appropriate text.

Level 1 provides the most support through repetition of high-frequency words, light text, predictable sentence patterns, and strong visual support.

Level 2 offers early readers a bit more challenge through varied simple sentences, increased text load, and less repetition of high-frequency words.

Level 3 advances early-fluent readers toward fluency through increased text and concept load, less reliance on visuals, longer sentences, and more literary language.

Level 4 builds reading stamina by providing more text per page, increased use of punctuation, greater variation in sentence patterns, and increasingly challenging vocabulary.

Level 5 encourages children to move from "learning to read" to "reading to learn" by providing even more text, varied writing styles, and less familiar topics.

Whichever book is right for your reader, Blastoff! Readers are the perfect books to build confidence and encourage a love of reading that will last a lifetime!

This edition first published in 2016 by Bellwether Media, Inc.

No part of this publication may be reproduced in whole or in part without written permission of the publisher. For information regarding permission, write to Bellwether Media, Inc., Attention: Permissions Department, 5357 Penn Avenue South, Minneapolis, MN 55419.

Library of Congress Cataloging-in-Publication Data

Schuetz, Kari.
  Charles Schulz / by Kari Schuetz.
    pages cm. – (Blastoff! Readers: Children's Storytellers)
  Summary: "Simple text and full-color photography introduce readers to Charles Schulz. Developed by literacy experts for students in kindergarten through third grade"– Provided by publisher.
  Includes bibliographical references and index.
  Audience: Ages 5-8
  Audience: K to grade 3
  ISBN 978-1-62617-264-7 (hardcover: alk. paper)
  1. Schulz, Charles M. (Charles Monroe), 1922-2000–Juvenile literature. 2. Cartoonists–United States–Biography–Juvenile literature. I. Title.
  PN6727.S3Z84 2016
  741.5'6973–dc23
  [B]
                              2015010987

Printed in the United States of America, North Mankato, MN.

Table of
Contents

Charles Schulz is one of the most celebrated **cartoonists** of all time. He is the man behind Charlie Brown, Snoopy, and the rest of the *Peanuts* gang.

For 50 years, Charles brought his young characters to life in his famous **comic strip**. His funny stories about them still **circulate** in newspapers and entertain readers of all ages.

A Growing Cartoonist

Charles Schulz was born in Minneapolis, Minnesota, on November 26, 1922. Most of his childhood years were spent in nearby St. Paul. His dad owned a barbershop there.

"The only thing I ever wanted to be was a cartoonist. That's my life. Drawing."
Charles Schulz

Minneapolis, Minnesota

fun fact

Pet dogs ran around the family home. Charles based Snoopy after a dog named Spike.

Growing up, Charles read newspaper comics with his dad. He loved the funnies so much that being an artist became his dream. He drew a lot to practice.

Charles always put more effort into drawing than schoolwork. Near the end of high school, he took his first drawing class at a local art school.

"To me it was not a matter of how I became a cartoonist but a matter of when."
Charles Schulz

fun fact

Hockey was Charles's other favorite hobby. He spent a lot of time playing the sport with friends.

After graduation, Charles tried to get magazines to **publish** his cartoons. He had no luck. To make money, he worked part-time jobs. He was a **golf caddy** and a delivery boy.

After World War II began, the United States Army **drafted** Charles. He did not let this stop him from drawing. He sketched pictures of his military camp.

When the war ended, Charles went to teach at his old art school. He worked there for five years while he drew his own cartoons.

"I would draw comic strips even if I weren't getting paid for it... I'm obsessed with thinking of funny things."
Charles Schulz

11

Peanuts Becomes Popular

Charles's big break came in 1947. The *St. Paul Pioneer Press* started publishing his *Li'l Folks* comics every week.

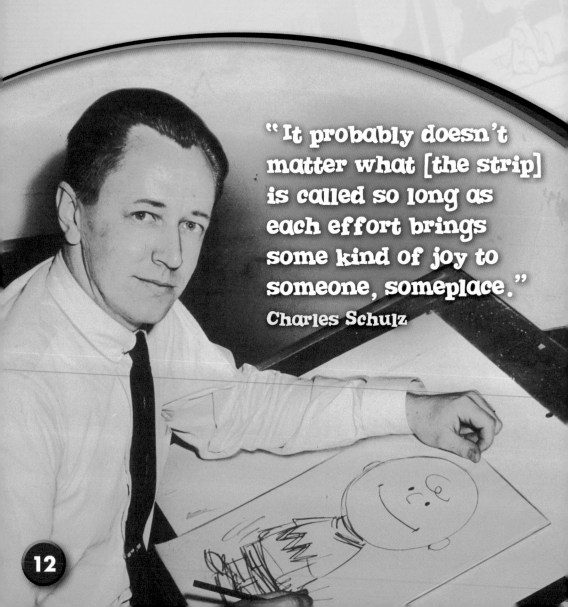

"It probably doesn't matter what [the strip] is called so long as each effort brings some kind of joy to someone, someplace."
Charles Schulz

Three years later, *Li'l Folks* appeared in seven newspapers across the country. By that time, it was called *Peanuts*. *Li'l Folks* was too close to the name of another comic strip.

Peanuts became a hit because the art was simple. Charles limited the lines he used and made each one count. This allowed the strip to stand out from others with highly decorated scenes.

Charles focused on the faces of his characters. Their heads were huge in size. Their expressions could show a lot of emotion.

The *Peanuts* characters were **relatable**. Charles made the group of friends like himself and people he knew. He gave each character a unique personality and way of looking at the world.

the *Peanuts* gang

Pigpen   Schroeder   Franklin   Sally   Marcie

Peppermint   Linus   Charlie   Woodstock
Patty   Brown

Snoopy   Lucy

! fun fact

Charles added the character Franklin in 1968. This was to support African Americans in their fight for equal rights.

SELECTED WORKS

Peanuts newspaper comics (1950-2000)

Selected *Peanuts* Books
Happiness Is a Warm Puppy (1962)
Security Is a Thumb and a Blanket (1963)
Love Is Walking Hand in Hand (1965)
Kick the Ball, Marcie! (1996)
Your Dog Plays Hockey? (1996)

Selected *Peanuts* Television Specials
A Charlie Brown Christmas (1965)
It's the Great Pumpkin, Charlie Brown (1966)
A Charlie Brown Thanksgiving (1973)

Readers came to care about what the *Peanuts* gang had to say. The group shared important messages about love, friendship, disappointment, and more.

The *Peanuts* characters quickly became **celebrities**. They started to appear on **advertisements**, Hallmark greeting cards, and in the Macy's Thanksgiving Day Parade. **NASA** made Snoopy the face of a safety program.

Charles also featured his gang in books and **animated** television specials.

POP CULTURE CONNECTION

A Charlie Brown Christmas is a *Peanuts* television special. It airs every year in the United States. The popular holiday feature has won an Emmy Award and a Peabody Award.

PEANUTS CLASSIC

A Charlie Brown Christmas

Bonus Feature Included! It's Christmastime Again, Charlie Brown

40 YEARS A Charlie Brown Christmas

Emmy® and Peabody Award Winner!

fun fact

More recently, artists have turned the *Peanuts* gang into large street statues in Minnesota and California.

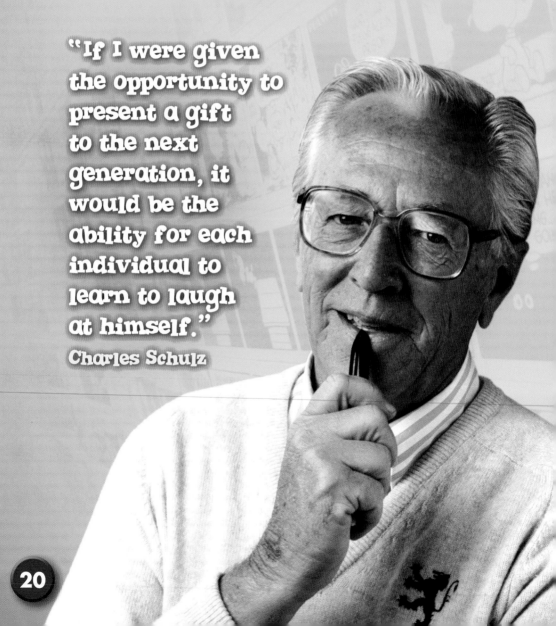

Over the years, Charles received many honors for his storytelling. He was named Outstanding Cartoonist of the Year twice. In 1999, he received an award for his life's work.

"If I were given the opportunity to present a gift to the next generation, it would be the ability for each individual to learn to laugh at himself."
Charles Schulz

IMPORTANT DATES

1922: Charles Schulz is born on November 26.

1947: *Li'l Folks* starts appearing every week in the *St. Paul Pioneer Press*.

1950: *Peanuts* is first published in newspapers across the country.

1955: The National Cartoonists Society gives Charles his first Outstanding Cartoonist of the Year award.

1964: Charles is named Outstanding Cartoonist of the Year for a second time.

1965: *A Charlie Brown Christmas* airs on television for the first time.

1967: The musical *You're a Good Man, Charlie Brown* first hits the theater.

1996: A star for Charles is added to the Hollywood Walk of Fame.

1999: The National Cartoonists Society gives Charles an award for his career.

2000: Charles passes away on February 12.

Charles passed away in 2000. However, today's readers still have his 17,897 *Peanuts* strips. With the collection, Charles created one of the longest stories ever told!

Glossary

advertisements—visuals that make people aware of products and programs

animated—quickly showing a series of drawings to create movement

cartoonists—artists who draw funny pictures to tell stories

celebrities—famous people

circulate—to be passed around between people

comic strip—a brief series of drawings in panels that are funny or that tell a story

drafted—called to military service

golf caddy—a person who carries a golfer's bag and clubs around a course

NASA—the National Aeronautics and Space Administration

publish—to print someone's work for a public audience

relatable—easy to connect with and understand

To Learn More

AT THE LIBRARY
Gherman, Beverly. *Sparky: The Life and Art of Charles Schulz*. San Francisco, Calif.: Chronicle Books, 2010.

Schulz, Charles M. *Charlie Brown and Friends: A Peanuts Collection*. Kansas City, Mo.: Andrews McMeel Publishing, 2014.

Schulz, Charles M. *Meet the Peanuts Gang!: With Fun Facts, Trivia, Comics, and More!* New York, N.Y.: Simon Spotlight, 2015.

ON THE WEB
Learning more about Charles Schulz is as easy as 1, 2, 3.

1. Go to www.factsurfer.com.

2. Enter "Charles Schulz" into the search box.

3. Click the "Surf" button and you will see a list of related web sites.

With factsurfer.com, finding more information is just a click away.

Index